INCREASING
AWARENESS

POCKET EDITION

Published from
Mardukite Borsippa HQ, San Luis Valley, Colorado
Mardukite Academy & Systemology Society
for spiritual or educational purposes only

INCREASING AWARENESS

Systemology
Professional Course
Booklet #1

Developed by Joshua Free
for the Systemology Society

© 2023, JOSHUA FREE

ISBN : 978-1-961509-25-2

Pocket Paperback Edition — *October 2023*

mardukite.com

Learn to Fly...

Then Chart Your Flight For Ascension!

Unlock your ultimate spiritual potential by removing barriers to your true native state.

Learn how to easily attain Self-actualization and help to actualize others along the way.

A greater appreciation and understanding of *Spiritual Life* and *Existence* awaits you. Expand your reach to achieve your dreams.

Each 'Professional Course' lesson-booklet offers simple exercises and techniques that directly apply the philosophy of Systemology, assisting to increase your true knowingness, improve your capabilities in this life, and even decide what you will do in your next.

At the Mardukite Academy of Systemology, the 'Professional Course' lessons in this series are presented to Seeker's that have completed the 'Basic Course', previously released as six lesson-booklets, or the six-in-one single volume edition "Fundamentals of Systemology."

This new presentation of the Systemology "Pathway-to-Ascension" takes Seekers from "Zero" to "Infinity" at lightning-fast speeds!

Discover who you really are...

Because you were never human

TABLET OF CONTENTS

PROFESSIONAL
COURSE
INTRODUCTION

WELCOME, SEEKER!
LET'S CHART YOUR JOURNEY
ON THE PATHWAY

Systemology is a "holistic" approach to understanding the human experience. It is not actually a singular "subject" in itself, but rather, a new way in which to view the many subjects of *Life* and all *Existence*.

This is a professional course in *Systemology*—specifically, how to *apply* the spiritual philosophy of *Mardukite Systemology* as a personal *"Pathway" to Ascension.* Our *Systemology* is a new approach to *"Self-Actualization."* It is completely relevant for the modern age and the future; and quite different from any previous similar attempts, or other traditions, you might find. What's more: it is applicable to anyone with any background.

This *"Professional Course"* series of lessons (booklets) immediately follows the material given in the *"Basic Course"* series— available as six separate pocket-sized booklets, or in a single hardcover volume titled: *"Fundamentals of Systemology: A New Thought For The 21st Century."*

This is a *new* presentation of *Systemology*, emphasizing the application of our philosophy for those *Seekers* that are *"Flying-Solo"*—or else working through their studies and exercises as solitary practitioners. This is a new innovation for *Systemology*. Aside from the book *"Crystal Clear,"* all of our former advanced courses have placed a focus on *"Traditional Piloting"*—where experienced practitioners assist *Seekers* in *"processing."*

To receive the greatest benefit from this study: it is expected that a *Seeker* will already be familiar with the fundamental concepts and terminology (previously relayed in the *Basic Course*) before using lessons from the *Professional Course*. This will allow us to cover the extensive territory of the *Pathway* much more quickly. However, for reference, a basic "*glossary*" of vocabulary used in this lesson is provided in the "*appendix*."

A NEW VIEW OF THE HUMAN SPIRIT

Systemology is not a religion and does not require any type of *faith*. It is, however, built upon a "spiritual" premise—and as such is an "applied spiritual philosophy." It is based on ancient teachings that we are *Spiritual Beings* essentially "wearing" bodies like clothes—or using them as "vehicles." Yet our true native nature is not *physical*, but beyond this existence; and we can certainly operate a "body" from *outside* of it.

We are **all** *Spiritual Beings*—each of us a *unit* of *Spiritual Awareness*—that have experienced a very long *Spiritual Timeline* of existence. Although we might be particularly attached to the familiar "physical shells" associated with *this* lifetime, our true *"Spiritual Lifetime"* is seemingly *eternal*. We have been many things before *Human*, and we go onward as a *Spiritual Being* after our *"genetic vehicle"* of *this* incarnation perishes.

While a "spiritual" view of the *Human Condition* may not seem unique to our philosophy, just how often is the concept treated *systematically*? For that matter: just how many people, supposedly raised to this or that religion, or professing to believe one thing or another, actually live their lives as though they are *Spirits?*

As *Spiritual Beings* of immortal existence and infinite potential, we are not simply the *"creations"* of an even greater *Being-*

ness; we are, in fact, an integral part of that *"creative force"* which permeates all existence.

Our basic nature is to be a *"creative being"*—our highest goals are *"to create."* And as such a being—which we refer to as an *Alpha-Spirit* in *Systemology*—we have run into some difficulties along the course of our *Spiritual Timeline* and found ourselves trapped within material *Universes* of our own collaborative *creation*.

Since we did not start out our existence in a trapped condition, it is correct to say that we have *"fallen"* from our native *"godlike"* states. It did not happen all at one, but progressively and systematically. We know our "troubles" have resulted from accumulated "barriers" and "blockages"—or *fragmentation*—during our vast experiences as *Spiritual Beings*. They are not because we lack something; but because of what's been added.

In *Systemology*, we systematically examine those routes by which we must have descended to reach our present condition, then reverse the direction of travel and chart a personal *"Pathway to Ascension."* Of course, the exact "details" of the *Spiritual Timeline* will be different for each individual *Seeker*. However, we have been able to systematically chart our *Pathway* based on common patterns of *Human fragmentation*.

In the most basic terms: the *fragmentation* that defines our "downward spiral" consists of decisions or considerations where we deny our true nature. This includes those decisions to *"withdraw"* rather than *"reach"*; where we choose to *not-know* rather than *know*; to *not-communicate* rather than *communicate*; and ultimately, to take *no-responsibility* for being a *creative-cause*, and therefore succumb to being an *effect*.

But there is *hope!* And much more importantly: there is an effectively workable *way out* of the mazes and traps of our existence. If you are reading this now, you have already begun to gather your tools and build up the *"horsepower"* necessary to break the gravity holding your *Spiritual Beingness* to the *Human Condition.*

STUDYING THE PROFESSIONAL COURSE

Most *Seekers* study and practice *Systemology* at-a-distance and independent of the "Mardukite Academy" or any "Master-level" mentors trained therein. This means that the *books* (and to a lesser degree, the *internet*) are the only means of direct contact a *Seeker* maintains with the "Systemology Society" during their studies. A continuing *Seeker* from the *"Basic Course"* will be familiar with the style of study found in *this* course.

Misunderstood words are the most common reason an individual abandons studying a subject. When a misunderstanding occurs, *Awareness* declines. These misunderstandings start to "stack up" after the first occurrence, and as a result, the level of interest and attention will also decline. This is how a "confusion" develops; and the individual will get "bored" with the subject, feel tired, and unable to concentrate.

One solution is to return to the part of the material that was still interesting and enjoyable to read. When scanning around that area of text, there is likely to be a new word (or new specific use of a familiar word) that is unclear, but was passed by unnoticed. All *Systemology* books include their own *glossary*. Using this *glossary* and a high-quality dictionary will help resolve this misunderstanding once it is located.

An effective education of any subject is taught on a *gradient*. This is what is intended by presenting the study of something as *"grades."* Rather than treating a subject as one total mass, true learning is achieved by increasing one's understanding with a *gradual* increase upward. The *ascent* to a mountaintop is not successfully achieved in one leap, but by targeting and reaching specific checkpoints along the way.

This *Professional Course* consists of a series of lessons (booklets) that gradually increase a *Seeker's* ability to understand and apply the practices and techniques of *Systemology* as a complete *"Pathway to Ascension."* It is an appropriate study for continuing *Seekers* (from the *Basic Course*), but also "advanced" *Systemologists*.

Each lesson (booklet) of the *Professional Course* applies *Systemology* to a particular subject (or focus). It is best if the entire course can be studied and applied in sequential order. These lessons also employ a style of practice or technique called *"Systematic Processing."* An introduction to applying this methodology is provided in the final lesson (booklet) of the *Basic Course*—or in the *"Fundamentals of Systemology"* volume.

To study the *Professional Course* just like a student at the Academy: a *Seeker* reads through all instructional material and applies each exercise (or *"process"*) presented in the text to the extent they comfortably can, before continuing on to the next lesson (booklet).

When first starting on the *Pathway* as a *Solo* practitioner, without the aid of an experienced *Pilot*, a *Seeker* shouldn't "push too hard" or allow themselves to get too "stuck" on any one area (lesson) or *process*. It is not expected that any one area will be completely handled when first introduced. For optimum results, it is expected that a serious *Seeker* will make more than one "pass" through the entire *Professional Course.*

The *Professional Course* is not altogether different from other forms of practical or technical education: where the instruction and exercises are delivered to a completion, and then a student further increases their abilities, strength and skill-level by applying additional practice throughout their life. Therefore, a student should not concern themselves with perfectly mastering each step (or lesson) before progressing forward.

Additional passes through the material are likely to result in different *"realizations"* (an increased *level of understanding*) than a previous time. New "layers" of *Knowingness* may now be accessible during a *process* that may not have been before. It is important to avoid invalidating the progress you've made just because one area is not completely handled right away, or if a certain *process* seems too difficult on the first pass.

CHARTING A COURSE ON
THE PATHWAY

Although we can communicate a systematic structure to *fragmentation,* the personal journey experienced along the *Pathway* will be different for each *Seeker.* For example, certain areas will seem more *"turbulent"* or difficult for one *Seeker* than another. We tend to say that these areas have more *"charge"* on them—or that they are more *"heavily charged."* It is best to handle such areas when you are already feeling "good" and not in a situation (or condition) where that specific area is consistently being *"triggered"* or *"restimulated."*

As an applied philosophy, *Systemology* "theory" can be easily utilized in the "laboratory" of the "world-at-large" in everyday life. This is implied within the basic instruction of each lesson. Unlike other "sciences" that conduct experiments by making a change to some "objective variable" *out there* and waiting to see an effect, our focus is the individual (or *Observer*) themselves, and how *they* affect the "*Reality*" perceived.

In addition to applying *Systemology* "New Thought" to everyday life, our philosophy is applied by using specific exercises and systematic techniques. These "*processes*" provide the most stable personal gain (and *realizations*) for each area; but only when actually applied with a *Seeker's* full "*presence*" and *Awareness*.

This *Professional Course* is designed so that it may be easily read and studied with little concern for what "dangers" these teachings—or *processing*—might unleash. However, there are still some guidelines that pertain to the "best-uses" of these course lessons, particularly if a *Seeker* intends for stable development.

Skipping over too much material/*processing* in early lessons may make attempts to understand (or apply) later lessons more difficult. However, once the complete *Professional Course* is worked through at least once in its entirety, specific areas can then be later returned to and treated with a greater sense of *Awareness* and *"presence"* than before. Of course, in *"Traditional Piloting,"* the rate of processing is monitored by an experienced practitioner; but in *"Solo-Processing,"* a *Seeker* must regulate their own progress on the *Pathway*.

Applying a systematic technique is called *"running a process."* The *processes* are designed with very simple instructions or "*command-lines*." To *run* a *processing command-line*, a *Seeker* may be assisted by the communication of that *line* from a "*Co-Pilot*" (as in "*Traditional Piloting*"). But even then, a *Seeker* must still personally "input" the *command* as *Self*. For this reason — and quite thankfully — *Solo-Processing* is possible.

TAKING FLIGHT ON THE PATHWAY

Processing Techniques are intended to treat the *Spiritual Being* or *Alpha-Spirit*; the individual themselves. It is applied by the *Alpha-Spirit* — then *Self-directed* to the "Mind-System" or even a "body" (*genetic-vehicle*), both of which are "constructs" that the *Alpha-Spirit* (*Self*, or the "I-AM" *Awareness unit*) operates, but neither of which is actually *Self*. *Fragmentation* causes *Humans* to falsely identify *Self as* the "*Mind*" or even a "*Body*."

The *Professional Course* lessons (booklets) are designed for the *Beginning Seeker* in mind—one that may have an understanding of theory, but with little experience in practice. That being said: each of these lessons may be used toward total *Beta-Defragmentation* within a specific area. There are also more *processes* given for each subject than may be necessary to achieve an *ultimate end-point realization* on that entire area.

Some *processes* can be treated quite lightly at first; others may require a bit of working at in order to get *"running"* well. It is important to set aside a period of time when you can be dedicated to your studies and *processing*. This period of time is referred to as a *"processing session."* The reason for this, is that when a *process* does start *running* well, it is important to be able to complete it to a satisfactory *"end-point."*

The purpose of *systematic processing* is to be able to *really* "look" at things and even determine the *considerations* we have made—or attitudes we have decided—about *Reality* as a result of those experiences. It doesn't do us much good to simply "glance"—or to *restimulate* something uncomfortable and then quickly *withdraw* from it once again, leaving more of our *attention* yet again behind and held fixedly on it.

Generally speaking, a *Seeker* continues to *run* a *process* so long as something is "happening"—which is to say, the *process* is still producing a change. Usually this is evident by the type of "answers" that a *command-line* helps a *Seeker* originate from the database of their own *Mind-System*. The *command-lines* do not "do" anything on their own. They assist a *Seeker* to direct their own attention toward increasing *Awareness*.

Of course, a *Seeker* may also cease to generate new "data" from a *process* without reaching an *"ultimate" realization* as an *"end-point."* It is possible that additional "layers" (or even other "areas") require handling before anything "deeper" is accessible. If this is the case, end the *process*. But, if a *Seeker* is *withdrawing* from something uncomfortable that was incited or stirred up, then a *process* is *run* until they feel "good" about it.

In case the thought of encountering *"turbulence"* is a concern: the techniques given as *"Opening Procedures"* of a *Formal Session* (in the *Basic Course*), and those found in the earliest lessons of the *Professional Course*, are quite useful when applied as "safety nets" for maintaining *Awareness* and *presence*, even when *Flying-Solo*.

One of the benefits to *Flying-Solo* is that *processing* is entirely *Self-determined*. This already provides a certain built-in "safety" for a practitioner. Anything you *restimulate* by *Self-determinism* is *your thing.* It is not incited by external *other-determined* influences (or other "source-points" in existence) that make you an *effect.* It can be more easily handled in *processing*—or you can simply let things "cool down" and come back to it again.

While it may seem "mysterious" to beginners, a *Seeker* gets a sense for knowing how long to *run* a *process* only with practice. Once you have spent some time actually applying the *Professional Course,* there are many aspects that become "second nature" because they are, in fact, a part of our true original nature. All we have done is *"reverse engineer"* the routes of *creation* and *consideration* that are already *our own.*

LESSON ONE:
INCREASING
AWARENESS

NEW SYSTEMATIC PROCESSES
INTRODUCED IN THIS LESSON

- Objective Universe Processing
- Orientation in Present Space-Time
  (*"Presence"*)
- Control of the Mind-Body Connection
- *"Touch-and-Let-Go"* (*"Touch-and-Go"*)
- Mental Reach
- Willingness to Reach
- *"Touch-Back"*
- *"The Wall"*

EXISTING PROCEDURES
DISCUSSED IN THIS LESSON

- The Formal Session (*Basic Course*)

FIRST FLIGHTS ON THE PATHWAY

"Processes" are systematic techniques—or *actions*—that are repeated toward a specific *end-point* or result. In most cases, they consist of a repetitive instruction—or *"command-line"*—that is *run* over and over until something happens. This is what produces a *realization*, which may not happen the first few *runs*. The same idea applies to hammering a nail with multiple strikes rather than simply pushing hard against it.

The first lessons (booklets) of the *Professional Course* are in some ways a review of many of the *techniques* introduced in the *Basic Course*. However, in this course, we will examine them much further as *processing* applications. In the *Basic Course*, just a few of the most critical *processes* are given as light *exercises* to supplement introductory lessons on the fundamental theory and philosophy of *Systemology*.

Much of the basic theory behind "*Systematic Processing*" may be found in *Lesson #6* of the *Basic Course*. In this *Professional Course*, we will be handling the *processes* directly as applications of our philosophy —and as a practical approach to unfolding the essential map of the *Pathway*, as researched by the *Systemology Society*.

SELF-DIRECTING ATTENTION

Consider for a moment that an *Alpha-Spirit* is able to *Self-direct* its nearly unlimited *Awareness*—and this has taken place across a long span of perceived existence (that we refer to as a *Spiritual Timeline*). Although the potential *Awareness* seems without limit, the ability to *handle* it has actually deteriorated over time, and with it, the potential "considerations" an *Alpha-Spirit* maintains of its own *Beingness*.

Understand that the original potential is *not* truly lost to us. It has, however, become *fragmented*. And by this, we mean that an individual's *attention* gets drawn toward painful instances and dangerous circumstances—and other "human problems" that can "fix" our *attention*. This, in fact, lowers the total *Awareness* immediately available to us; it affects just how much of our true *Self-determinism* is "in play."

Systematic Processing, in general, is an exercise in "*selectively directing attention.*" This is one of the reasons it is so effective for increasing *Awareness*. The exercises given in the *Basic Course*—particularly those related to "*presence in-session*" or the *Opening Procedures* for a *Formal Session*—are the most fundamental *processes* by themselves, because they "orient" a

Seeker in present time and space to make any other *processing* workable.

Our *processing* methods are effective when they can collect (or concentrate) a *Seeker's* available *Awareness* (or "actualized" *Awareness*) and then increase it. This is essentially the *opposite* of hypnotism. In *processing*, a *Seeker* "frees up" more of their available *"attention units"* by taking them off of whatever they have been fixed on *unknowingly* throughout one's existence. These *"units"* have gotten stuck on things along the way.

"Fragmentation" is an archaic systemological term we still use today because it implies a "dispersal" of energy—or quite literally the "fracture" of a wholeness or totality into many parts. It is meant that some *thing* is in the way of a "clear view" (or "clear communication").

In most cases, *fragmentation* concerns what we don't want to confront directly

—so we kind of "shut down" on those areas and withdraw, but without actually taking all of our *attention units* off of it. We don't really want to deal with it, but we can't trust it not to "bite" us when we're not looking. This "area" sinks into the shadowy gray parts of our *Awareness* until it becomes completely handled *unknowingly* "on automatic."

We have also retained the word "*imprint.*" This is best understood in this wise: you may have noticed that you are likely to give something more *attention* when it is first encountered—and certainly, common language makes frequent use of the phrase "*first impression.*" It is at these instances that we essentially take the data we have received and duplicate it as our own *Reality.* And this is what we agree to as *being Reality.*

When an *Alpha-Spirit* stops "*looking*" and "*creating,*" and starts using *imprinting* as the basis of *Reality*, the total available *Awareness* declines. The individual is still carrying the same amount of *Spiritual Awareness Energy* (or *ZU*) as they always have—but these energy stores have become increasingly "solidified." The heavier or more solid these energy units are, the farther below the line of *Actualized Awareness* they sink.

For *processing* to be effective, we begin with those *techniques* that will bring together those "*attention units*" that *are* actually accessible to a *Seeker*. These are also useful as general methods for "*selectively directing attention*" on other tasks, or in times of mental or emotional strain. "Orientation in Present Space-Time" is also a critical part of the *Standard Opening Procedures* for a *Formal Session*.

The alternating "*command-lines*" in the sample script for a *Formal Session* (as given in the *Basic Course*), are:

"Look around and spot something in the room."

"What do you notice about that?"

Of course, this is taken from a *"Traditional Piloting"* transcript, which involves two individuals—a *Pilot* and a *Seeker*—and is dependent on their relay of communication. Many variations of this are effective. An alternative *processing command-line* (or *"PCL"*) that may be more applicable for *"Solo-Processing"* (rather than the communicative approach), is:

"Look around and notice things. Locate precise points on the object, moving quickly from one point to another."

In basic terms, this *knowingly* duplicates the original basic systematic process of *imprinting*. This is what we do when we encounter a new person or enter a new place—at least *before* we tend to leave our ability to *perceive* and *create* (or *duplicate*) on automatic. We take a permanent snap-shot to base our total *Reality*, but its vibrancy often fades. This is why the vividness of *Life* and the *Universe* can seem so "dull" sometimes.

Now, it is important when doing this *process* that you are actually "spotting precise points" with your full *attention* and not just casually glancing all about. Remember that these *are* "systematic processes" in spite of how plain the language used actually is, or how simple or trivial the action required may seem.

When using this *process* during periods of emotional turbulence or mental strain, you may suddenly feel more alert or clearer in your perceptions. Even if already awake and alert, there should be a sense of improvement, or perhaps the room may seem to be a little "brighter" than before. In either case, you would acknowledge (even to yourself, if *Flying-Solo*) that the *process* has reached a satisfactory "*end-point.*"

In addition to the improved "orientation in present space-time," this *process* also demonstrates the ability of the *Alpha-Spirit* to direct its *attention* and therefore control its experience of a mental state. Such is an example of a potential *"realization"* that might also spontaneously occur as a result of *running* this *process*.

ADVANCED APPLICATIONS

There are many applications for the previous *process* other than focusing *presence* for additional *processing*. In fact, early experiments with *"presence"* led to an entire route of advanced work (otherwise referred to as "A.T.") regarding *perception* of —and *operation* in—existence as an *Alpha-Spirit*, but independent of *any* body. Such is the *true* native state of *Self*.

41

This more advanced subject is presently brought up because of its ability to illustrate just how "not-trivial" the previous *process* really is. This became evident when *Seekers* assisting with research at the *Systemology Society* began to experiment with the previous *process*, but with their *eyes closed*.

Whether eyes are open or closed, this type of technique is called *"objective processing"* because it pertains directly to the "objective environment" or *Physical Universe (Beta-Existence)*. This is quite different from a *"subjective process"* that calls for a *Seeker* to "remember" or "consider" something. There are other types, but the majority fall within either of these two categories.

If a *Seeker* wishes to experiment with the advanced version: start with the previous *process* as given while seated comfortably in a room. Once you have reached an *end-point* with that, close your eyes and repeat the *process* using an "imaginary" view of the room.

This practice is best done without straining and without concerns about accuracy. It is important, especially early on the *Pathway*, to acknowledge every "win" without invalidating a level of ability not yet regained. A *Seeker* should also avoid repeatedly opening their eyes to "check" whether or not their personal "copy" fits what is otherwise viewable with the body's eyes.

When first practicing with a technique like this, there are likely to be a lot of gaps of *real perception* filled-in with "created" or "imagined" scenery. Much of it will not necessarily be a one-to-one duplicate of what the body sees. It is also possible to perceive things that *are* "real," which the body is not able to sense.

Although presented early in our instruct-

43

ional lessons, this version is actually part of the advanced *processes* because its application is not restricted to standard "*defragmentation*" procedures. It is just one example of the *processing* we treat in this *Professional Course* that continues to be practiced at "advanced levels." It does not particularly have a "finite" *end-point* when applied during this lifetime.

Another application of this formula is to *knowingly* focus *attention* on specific points of the body (or *genetic-vehicle*). There is a tendency to operate the body on "auto-pilot." Often, our *attention* "snaps-in" on the body rather violently during painful incidents—and *then* we are suddenly *very aware* of it. The lack of *Self-determinism* involved in this abrupt shift in *Awareness* only reinforces the falsehood that we *are* our bodies.

HELPFUL TIPS ON PROCESSING

The second *process* we will introduce in
the *Professional Course* is also an integral
part of *Opening Procedures*. It is part of a
cycle referred to as "Command of the
Mind-Body Connection." Where we previously have *knowingly Self-directed* our
attention to "spot" things, we now make
deliberately intended actions to both
"reach" and "withdraw" from them. This
will also allow for additional training on
general *processing*.

Perhaps one of the more challenging aspects for beginners to grasp about *processing,* is knowing just how long to *run* a
process for. There is, of course, a liability
to either *running* a *process* too long or not
long enough.

For example: if a *process* is left as an in-
complete cycle, a *Seeker* does not earn the

gains or new *realizations* they otherwise would—and they likely have left a bit of *attention* on something stirred up, but not handled. On the other hand: if a *process* is run too long, a *Seeker* may start to feel tired (or "heavy")—the actual end-point when they felt better from the *process* was missed or unacknowledged.

There is much less liability—and by this, we mean the chance of hindrance of progress on the *Pathway*—by experimenting with "*overrun*" and "*underrun*" on these more fundamental "*objective processes*." Getting a "sense" for this early on the *Pathway* allows greater certainty in handling more intensive *processing* further along. This is of tremendous importance for *Seekers* intending to *Solo-Pilot* the entire *Professional Course*.

This *process* immediately follows the previous one in the *Standard Opening Procedures* of a *Formal Session* because it builds on the *presence* and *certainty* already established. In order to "touch" and "let go" of an object, a *Seeker* must first "spot" the object in present space-time. This may seem like only a slight increase or gradual incline in the "challenge" or "difficulty level" presented to a *Seeker*—and rightfully so. Much of the stable progress earned along the *Pathway* will be attained this way.

The repetitive alternating *"processing command-lines"* ("PCL") given in the sample script for a *Formal Session* are:

"(Choose an object.) Decide you are going to reach for it; then make that body pick it up."

"Now decide when you are going to put it down and make that body put it back where it was."

Usually, once a specific object is chosen, the *process* is *run* on that same item repetitively. While this example is quite direct, there are many PCL variations that could be just as effectively applied. What's given above is not even the most basic form of this *process*, which is:

"*(Choose an object.) Decide on an exact spot on the object and reach for it.*"

"*Now touch that spot for a moment; and then let go of it.*"

This is repeated over and over quite a few times. In addition to its use as a preliminary to a *Formal Session*, typically a *process* such as this is *run* in order for a *Seeker* to actually learn something, or come to a "new" *realization*. This is always our intention for *processing*; but in this case, it is to *realize* the level of "command" an individual directly has over the behaviors of their *Body* and functions of the *Mind*.

Putting the *realizations* of this specific *process* aside for a moment, let us use it to demonstrate *running* a *process* in general. For one thing: a continuing *Seeker* (from the *Basic Course*) with an understanding of the *"Beta-Awareness Scale"* (detailing a sequential range of emotions and mental states) may notice that an individual often comes *up* from the *bottom* of the scale during a *process*.

It requires a bit of *Self-determination* to get started on a *process* and quite a bit more to continue *running* it. In this example, it takes some time *running* to get past the immediate feeling of *"So what?"* or *"I touch things all the time."* After further *running*, perhaps the attitude rises on the scale to *"This is stupid"* or *"This is boring."* But if you push through this, a *Seeker* gets interested and starts to feel better and the object seems brighter. ***This*** is when you have reached an *end-point* on the *process*.

"Underrun" would be anything short of the *end-point* (such as the other states or attitudes just described). However, if you want to get a sense of *"overrun,"* you can experiment with this same *process* by con-

tinuing it longer, past the appropriate *end-point* when you were feeling good about it. The longer you continue to *run* it, the further back down the *Beta-Awareness Scale* you may find yourself slipping; feeling worse about it and finding the repetition less tolerable and more difficult to handle than before.

Such *"overrun"* can easily take place during *processing*, when an *end-point* is not acknowledged (and the *process* is not stopped). In *"Traditional Piloting,"* it is up to an experienced practitioner to recognize these points—but when *Flying-Solo*, a *Seeker* should get familiar with this phenomenon and know how to fix it.

The basic pattern observed of *overrun* is: a *process* begins "rough," then suddenly it "smooths" out and seems easy and fun (which is the *release-point* or *end-point*), and then it starts to feel "tough" again to continue doing. In this case, a *Pilot* has "flown past" or "bypassed" the appropriate "landing spot."

The most basic solution to *overrunning* a *process* is simply to "spot" the exact moment when you were feeling good and *did* reach an *end-point*. By "spot," we mean to definitively notice or perceive something distinctively—and not necessarily visually or with the eyes. If you can bring to mind the instance when you were feeling good about the object, then it should start to seem that way again.

At the other end of things, "*underrun*" is primarily a result of one's own premature *withdrawal* from the *process*. It only occurs by stopping a *process* before an *end-point* is reached. When not due to outside interruption, this usually happens when the content or data addressed by a *process* causes discomfort.

In the example we have been using, there is very little mental strain or emotional turbulence attached to touching and letting go of an object in our surroundings —unless perhaps we have selected an object that we don't particularly *"like"* very much. But in later *processes*, once something is critically stirred up, it is important not to *withdraw* from it simply because it seems "difficult."

The "difficulties" initially encountered with handling something "turbulent" are much different than how things seem when something is *overrun*. For one thing: if a *process* is *underrun*, a *release-point* or *end-point* has not yet been reached. So we don't want to *withdraw* from a *process* just because it feels uncomfortable.

Therefore, if something is "happening" (*e.g.*, there is movement on the *Awareness Scale*) or a *process* has "triggered" or "turned on" a reactive-mechanism, the only systematic action is to continue *run-*

ning the *process* until the *end-point* is actually arrived at. This is why we use "*sessions*" to avoid outside influence; because if the present *restimulation* is due to the *process*, then continuing to *run* that *process* will handle it. And, of course, the moment it is actually *handled*—when you "feel good" about it—you *end* the *process*.

TOUCH-AND-LET-GO

We use the "*touch-and-let-go*" exercise as a training example at the *Mardukite Academy*, but it is also a real *process*. The standard version has already been relayed:

"Look around and choose an object."

"Now, choose a specific spot on the object."

"Touch and let go of it (until you feel good about it)."

*"Choose a different spot on the object; and do
the same."*

*"Do this on individual spots until the object
seems more acceptable to you."*

After having some practice with this *process* on many "spots" using various different objects, you can then apply this technique in everyday life with various things you find yourself using frequently. This is especially useful on "things at work"—and also on automobiles; everyone should be required to do this on vehicles before they are driven among other individuals.

As a variation of this (in *processing*), it is quite standard to have a *Seeker* "spotting spots" on "walls" of the *processing* room, and performing the same *"touch-and-let-go"* cycles. This not only increases personal *"presence"* (of *Awareness*) in present space-time, but also increases the vibrancy of the room. Using "walls" in this *process* enables directing *Awareness* on "spots" that are not part of objects or particularly interesting.

In a *Formal Session*, "*objective processing*" (such as this) is also applied in between the more "*introspective*" *processes*, in order to maintain a *Seeker*'s orientation (or "*presence*") of *Awareness* (in present space-time). This is particularly important during prolonged *intensive sessions* that include many individual *processes*.

Advanced applications of this basic "*touch-and-let-go*" technique require "mentally reaching out" with *attention* — or extending/projecting one's *Awareness* — like a beam of energy.

As with handling the very first process given in this lesson (booklet), you would practice by beginning with the "physical" version (and *running* it to an *end-point*) and then switch over to the "mental" one (using the same object). This would first be *run* with eyes open: *looking* at the object and mentally reaching—not just with your *attention*, but as if you are actually making "contact" (or "touching") the object. It can also be *run* with eyes closed.

Another advanced variation of this is applied to the *Standard Opening Procedures* of a *Formal Session*, when a *Seeker* is directed to:

"Close your eyes. Put all of your attention on the upper two back corners of the room and just get real interested in them for a while."

WILLINGNESS TO REACH

One reason we practice deliberate (*Self-determined*) and repetitive *"touch-and-go"* cycles is because so much of this activity in our lives becomes "automated" and "reactive." For example: if we touch a "hot" surface, the reflex to pull away (re-

tract or *withdraw*) is not *Self-determined*.
This lack of *Self-determinism* even contributes to prolonging the sense of "pain" we
may experience afterward.

One of the systematic techniques for
handling this, which can be used in
everyday life, is called the *"touch back."*
By this, we mean duplicating the action
that hurt you on your own *Self-determinism*. Of course, we mean to do this *slowly*
and *safely*. This should include repetitive
"touch-and-go" on various objects in the
location of the incident, in addition to
whatever caused the actual injury. But,
for example: in the case of a "hot stove,"
you would wait until it cooled; or you
would cover the edge of a "sharp" instru-
ment, *&tc.*

The automation or reactivity of a *"flinch"*
or *"withdrawal"* also involves a decrease
in *Actualized Awareness*. It is simply inher-
ent in the systematic mechanisms at
work. When you are hurt, *attention* may

"snap-in" on the body as an *effect*, but the actual *Self-determined Awareness* withdraws. Even with emergency medical attention, the "withdrawal" or "avoidance" of *Self-determining attention* on that area will inhibit healing. Most physicians will agree that beyond the medical care they can provide, the rest is the patient's attitude.

For example: even with something as simple as "stubbing your toe"—you may have noticed that the sting of the pain continues to hurt after the incident takes place; and for a surprisingly long time, given the lack of real damage that usually occurs. What's more: there is a tendency to "stub" the same toe again soon afterward, because we have also *withdrawn* our attention from the toe and prefer not to *confront* the event.

The short answer to this "mystery"—and most aspects of *defragmentation* in general—is *"Awareness."* An application of the "*touch back*" in the above example would be to *Self-determine* moving your foot slowly to lightly contact the surface you had hit.

The first time, the sharpness of the *restimulation* brings up to mind the original incident itself. But, after a few more *runs* of this *process*, the pain more quickly subsides (and there is less of a tendency for the same injury to repeat again). This is one example of applying *Systemology* philosophy to life that does not require a PCL or "*session*" to utilize—*although* specific instructions may be easily communicated if assisting another.

What we are starting to handle, in the long run, is the "*willingness to reach*"—and the more "physical" or "objective" exercises systematically *duplicate* the type of *mental processing* already taking place in the Mind. There is a tremendous amount of theory behind these techniques that is covered in the more advanced *Systemology* texts; but the *processes* given in this *Professional Course* speak volumes for themselves if applied.

THE WALL

The final *process* covered in this lesson (booklet) is deceptively simple to *run,* and is also popularly spoken of by *Mardukite Academy* students. There is always a lot of gossip and jokes concerning "*The Wall.*" This sometimes leads to not taking it seriously; but that is usually a result of not executing the actions in a fully *Self-determined* and precise manner. Each of the actions is made as if it is the *first time*; not simply a *repeat.*

The most basic PCL for this *process*:

"*Look at that wall.*"
"*Walk over to that wall.*"
"*Touch the wall.*"

"Turn around."

This *process* is *run* in an open room between two walls. It is important that there is a clear path between the walls. It is preferable if the walls are bare. It is done *over* and *over* again. There is a point when *running* this *process* can really *"ping"* you with some discomfort; it may even stir up a lot of sensations that stem from things that remain "beneath the surface" and not yet accessible. But push through any of this and continue. Whatever point you start to feel good about handling control of the *Body*, end the *process*.

As with other examples of *"objective processing,"* this may also be applied as an advanced "eyes-closed" *process*. In this case it is best if you can lie down comfortably on the floor. And again, as with the other examples, you would begin your practice with the standard version, physically walking between the two walls. Afterward, you perform the same deliberate PCL actions, but *imagining* yourself as a *Spirit* doing it.

The Systemology Professional Course
continues in the next lesson booklet:
THOUGHT & EMOTION

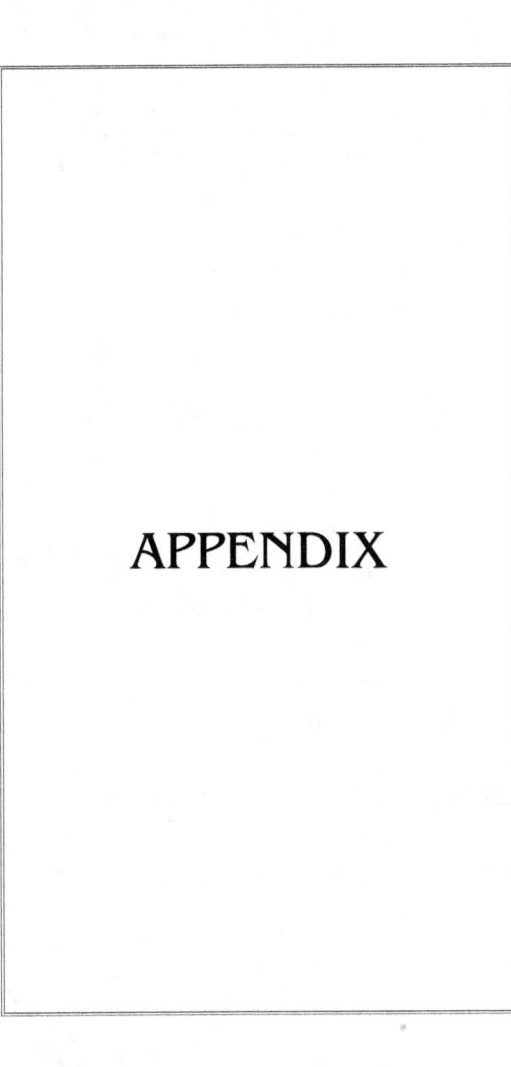

APPENDIX

APPENDIX A: BETA-AWARENESS

4.0 SELF-HONESTY (BETA)
3.9 "Vibrant" ("Charismatic")
3.8 "Enthusiastic" ("In Love")
3.7 "Energetic"
3.6 "Cheerful"
3.5 CONFIDENT ("Positive")
3.4 "Determined"
3.3 "Eager"
3.2 "Alert" ("Attentive")
3.1 "Strong Interest"
3.0 INTERESTED ("Content")
2.9 "Small Interest"
2.8 "Encouraged"
2.7 "Disinterested"
2.6 "Doubtful"
2.5 INDIFFERENT ("Tolerant")
2.4 "Bored"
2.3 "Dislike" ("Neglectful")
2.2 "Tired"
2.1 "Monotony"

2.0   INVALIDATING ("Pessimistic")

1.9   "Antagonism"

1.8   "Suffering" ("In Pain")

1.7   "Confrontational"

1.6   "Violent"

1.5   ANGRY ("Negative")

1.4   "Hateful"

1.3   "Spiteful"

1.2   "Resentment"

1.1   "Anxiety"

1.0   FEAR ("Afraid")

0.9   "Terror"

0.8   "Numb"

0.7   "Evasive"

0.6   "Loss"

0.5   GRIEF ("Sadness")

0.4   "Depression"

0.3   "Victimization"

0.2   "Hopelessness"

0.1   "Apathy" ("Unconsciousness")

0.0   BETA CONTINUITY (Organic Death)

APPENDIX B: THE FORMAL SESSION

1. <u>BEGINNING THE SESSION</u>

"Would it be okay with you if we begin this session now?"

"Okay."

"Start of session."

2. <u>OPENING PROCEDURES</u>

 A. Presence In-Session

"Is there anything going on that might keep your attention from being present in-session?"

 (if *"no,"* acknowledge and go to B.; if *"yes,"* continue below)

"Okay. Tell me about it."

"Alright. How does that problem seem to you now?"

 (if *"further away"* or handled, acknowledge and go to B.; if *"closer"* or more turbulent, continue below)

"*Spot something in the incident; Spot something in the room.*"

(this alternating command line is repeated as needed)

B. Orientation in Present Space-Time

"*Get the sense of you making that body sit in that chair.*"

"*Okay. Get a sense of the floor beneath your feet.*"

"*Do you have that real good?*"

(if "*no*," acknowledge and repeat *A.*; if "*yes*," continue below)

"*Recall a time something seemed real to you.*"

"*Tell me something you notice about it.*"

"*Look around and spot something in the room.*"

"*What do you notice about that?*"

(these last four command lines are repeated in series as needed; acknowledge and continue below)

C. Control of Body and Mind In-Session

(two dissimilar objects—here given as "Item-1" and "Item-2"—are presented and placed within reach; or alternatively, at two distant points in the room, in which a command line for "walking" between them would be inserted)

"Pick up Item-1."

"Tell me about its weight."

"Tell me about its color."

"Tell me about its texture."

"Put it down."

"Pick up Item-2."

"Tell me about its weight."

"Tell me about its color."

"Tell me about its texture."

"Put it down."

(this series of command-lines may be repeated several times; when there is no communication-lag for several full series, and duplicate answers are reoccurring, acknowledge and continue below)

"Choose an object. Decide when you are going to reach for it. Then make that body pick it up."

"Now decide when you are going to put it down. Then make that body put it back where it was."

(repeat as needed; when there is no communication-lag for a full series of command lines, acknowledge and continue below)

"Close your eyes. Put all of your attention on the upper two back corners of the room and just get real interested in them for a while."

(if there are no visible signs of "strain" after two minutes, acknowledge and continue below)

D. Establishing the Session

"Do you have any goals for this session, or anything in particular you want to address?"

(acknowledge, then start a process)

3. STARTING A PROCESS

"I would like to start a process; would that be okay?"

"Alright. The command lines are ---. Does this make sense?"

(if *"no,"* clear up any misunderstood words; if *"yes,"* start the process)

4. <u>CHANGING A PROCESS</u>

(only the wording in a command line may be changed to make it more workable for a *Seeker*; to change processes altogether, the present process must reach an end-point)

Example: a Seeker expresses inability to "imagine" or visualize imagery.

"Okay. Well, just 'get a sense' of..." or *"Just 'get the idea' of..."*

Example: a Seeker expresses discomfort (or withdrawal from) recalling a particular incident.

"That's fine. What part of that incident 'could' you confront?"

5. <u>STOPPING A PROCESS</u>

(when an end-point has been reached on a repetitive-style process)

70

"We'll just run this process a couple more times if that's okay with you?"

(general process is run two more times)

"Okay. Is there anything you would like to tell me before we end this process?"

(**or**, if an end-point "realization" is communicated from a process)

"Alright. Very good."

(the formal end of a particular process requires a command-line)

"End of process."

6. <u>ENDING THE SESSION</u>

(once a process, or series of processes, is completed)

"Is there anything you would like to tell me before we end this session?"

(if *"yes,"* acknowledge and handle it with communication before ending the session; if *"no,"* continue below)

"Would it be okay if we ended this session now?"

"Okay."

"End of session."

GLOSSARY

actualization : to make actual, not just potential; to bring into full solid Reality; to realize fully in *Awareness* as a "thing."

agreement (reality) : unanimity of opinion of what is "thought" to be known; an accepted arrangement of how things are; things we consider as "real" or as an "is" of "reality"; a consensus of what is real as made by standard-issue (common) participants; what an individual contributes to or accepts as "real"; in *Systemology*, a synonym for "*reality.*"

alpha : the first, primary, basic, superior or beginning of some form; in *Systemology*, referring to the state of existence operating on spiritual archetypes and postulates, will and intention "exterior" to the low-level condensation and solidity of energy and matter as the 'physical universe' (*beta*).

alpha-spirit : a "spiritual" *Life*-form; the "true" *Self* or I-AM; the *individual*; the spiritual (*alpha*) *Self* that is animating the (*beta*) physical body or "*genetic vehicle*" using a continuous *Lifeline* of spiritual ("*ZU*") energy; an individu-

73

al spiritual (*alpha*) entity possessing no physical mass or measurable waveform (motion) in the Physical Universe as itself, so it animates the (*beta*) physical body or "*genetic vehicle*" as a catalyst to experience *Self*-determined causality in effect within the *Physical Universe*; a singular unit or point of *Spiritual Awareness* that is *Aware* that it is *Aware*.

ascension : actualized *Awareness* elevated to the point of true "spiritual existence" exterior to *beta existence*. An "Ascended Master" is one who has returned to an incarnation on Earth as an inherently *Enlightened One*, demonstrable in their words and actions; they have the ability to *Self-direct* the "Mind" and "Body" as *Self* (as a "Spirit"); and to maintain consciousness as a personal identity continuum with the same *Self-directed* control and communication of Will-Intention that is exercised, actualized and developed deliberately during one's present incarnation.

attention : active use of *Awareness* toward a specific aspect or thing; the act of "attending" with the presence of *Self*; a direction of focus or concentration of *Awareness* along a particular channel or conduit or toward a particular terminal node or communication termination point; the Self-directed concentration of personal energy as a combination of observation, thought-waves and consideration; focused application of *Self-Directed Awareness*.

awareness : the highest sense of-and-as *Self* in knowing and being as I-AM (the *Alpha-Spirit*); the extent of beingness directed as a viewpoint (POV) experienced by *Self* as knowingness.

beta (existence) : all manifestation in the "Physical Universe" (KI, in *Zuism*); the "Physical" state of existence consisting of vibrations of physical energy and physical matter moving through physical space and experienced as "time"; the conditions of *Awareness* for the *Alpha-spirit* (*Self*) as a physical organic *Lifeform* or "*genetic vehicle*" in which it experiences causality in the *Physical Universe*.

charge : to fill or furnish with a quality; to supply with energy; to lay a command upon; in *Systemology*—to imbue with intention; to overspread with emotion; personal energy stores and significances entwined as fragmentation in mental images, reactive-response encoding and intellectual (and/or) programmed beliefs.

communication : successful transmission of information, data, energy (&tc.) along a message line, with a reception of feedback; an energetic flow of intention to cause an effect (or duplication) at a distance; the personal energy moved or acted upon by will or else 'selective directed attention'; the 'messenger action' used to transmit and receive energy across a medium; also relay of energy, a message or signal—or even locating a personal POV (viewpoint) for the Self—along the *ZU-line*.

defragmentation : the *reparation* of wholeness; collecting all dispersed parts to reform an original whole; a process of removing "*fragmentation*" in data or knowledge to provide a clear understanding; applying techniques and processes that promote a *holistic* interconnected *alpha* state, favoring observational *Awareness* of continuity in all spiritual and physical systems; in *Systemology*, a "*Seeker*" achieving actualized "*Self-Honest Awareness*" is said to be in a basic state of *beta-defragmentation*, whereas *Alpha-defragmentation* is the rehabilitation of the *creative ability*, managing the *Spiritual Timeline* and the POV of *Self* as Alpha-Spirit (I-AM).

fragmentation : breaking into parts and scattering the pieces; the *fractioning* of wholeness or the *fracture* of a holistic interconnected *alpha* state, favoring observational *Awareness* of perceived connectivity between parts; *discontinuity*; separation of a totality into parts; in *Systemology*, a person outside of *Self-Honesty* is said to be operating from a *fragmented* state.

genetic-vehicle : a physical *Life*-form; the physical (*beta*) body that is animated/controlled by the (*Alpha*) *Spirit* using a continuous *Spiritual Lifeline* (ZU); a physical (*beta*) organic receptacle and catalyst for the (*Alpha*) *Self* to operate "causes" and experience "effects" within the *Physical Universe*.

holistic : the examination of interconnected systems as encompassing something greater than the *sum* of their "parts."

Human Condition : a standard default state of Human experience that is generally accepted to be the extent of its potential identity (*beingness*) —currently treated as *Homo Sapiens Sapiens,* but which is scheduled for replacement by *Homo Novus* (the "New Human").

imprint : to strongly impress, stamp, mark (or outline) onto a softer 'impressible' substance; to mark with pressure onto a surface; in *Systemology*, the term is used to indicate permanent Reality impressions marked by frequencies, energies or interactions experienced during periods of emotional distress, pain, unconsciousness, loss, enforcement, or something antagonistic to physical (personal) survival, all of which are are stored with other reactive response-mechanisms at lower-levels of *Awareness* as opposed to the active memory database and proactive processing center of the Mind; an experiential "memory-set" that may later resurface—be triggered or stimulated artificially—as Reality, of which similar responses will be engaged automatically; holographic-like imagery "stamped" onto consciousness as composed of energetic *facets* tied to the "snap-shot" of an experience.

pilot : a professional steersman responsible for healthy functional operation of a ship toward a specific destination; in *Systemology*, an intensive trained individual qualified to specially apply *Systemology Processing* to assist other *Seekers* on the *Pathway*.

presence : the quality of some thing (energy/matter) being "present" in space-time; personal orientation of *Self* as an *Awareness* (*POV*) located in present space-time (environment) and communicating with extant energy-matter.

processing command line (PCL) or **command line** : a directed input; a specific command using highly selective language for *Systemology Processing*; a predetermined directive statement (cause) intended to focus concentrated attention (effect).

processing, systematic : the inner-workings or "through-put" result of systems; in *Systemology*, a method of applied spiritual technology used toward personal Self-Actualization; methods of selective directed attention, communicated language and associative imagery that increases personal control of the human condition.

realization : the clear perception of an understanding; a consideration or understanding on what is "actual"; to make "real" or give "reality" to so as to grant a property of "being-ness" or "being as it is"; the state or instance of coming to an *Awareness*; in *Systemology*, "gnosis" or true knowledge achieved during *systematic processing*; achievement of a new (or "higher") cognition, true knowledge or perception of Self; a consideration of reality or assignment of meaning.

responsibility : the *ability* to *respond*; the extent of mobilizing *power* and *understanding* an individual maintains as *Awareness* to enact *change*; the proactive ability to *Self-direct* and make decisions independent of an outside authority.

Seeker : an individual on the *Pathway to Self-Honesty*; a practitioner of *Mardukite Systemology* or *Systemology Processing*, that is working toward *Spiritual Ascension*.

79

Self-actualization : bringing the full potential of the Human spirit into Reality; expressing full capabilities and creativeness of the *Alpha-Spirit*.

Self-determinism : the freedom to act, clear of external control or influence; the personal control of Will to direct intention.

Self-honesty : the basic or original *alpha* state of *being* and *knowing*; clear and present total *Awareness* of-and-as *Self*, in its most basic and true proactive expression of itself as *Spirit* or *I-AM*—free of artificial attachments, perceptive filters and other emotionally-reactive or mentally-conditioned programming imposed on the human condition by the systematized physical world; the ability to experience existence without judgment.

spiritual timeline : a continuous stream of moment-to-moment *Mental Images* (or a record of experiences) that defines the "past" of a spiritual being (or *Alpha-Spirit*) and which includes impressions (*imprints, &tc.*) from all life-incarnations and significant spiritual events the being has encountered; in Systemology, also "*backtrack.*"

Systemology : a modern tradition of applied religious philosophy and spiritual technology based on *Arcane Tablets* (in combination with *"general systemology"* and *"games theory"*) developed in the New Age underground by Joshua Free in 2011 as an advanced futurist extension of the *Mardukite Research Org.*; also known as *"Mardukite Systemology," "Metahuman Systemology"* and *"Spiritual Systemology."*

turbulence : a quality or state of distortion or disturbance that creates irregularity of a flow or pattern; the quality or state of aberration on a line (such as ragged edges) or the emotional "turbulent feelings" attached to a particular flow or terminal node; a violent, haphazard or disharmonious commotion (such as in the ebb of gusts and lulls of wind action).

ZU : the ancient Sumerian cuneiform sign for the archaic verb—*"to know," "knowingness"* or *"awareness"*; in *Mardukite Zuism and Systemology*, the active energy/matter of the "Spiritual Universe" (AN) experienced as a *Lifeforce* or *consciousness* that imbues living forms extant in the "Physical Universe" (KI); *"Spiritual Life Energy"*; energy demonstrated by the WILL of an actualized *Alpha-Spirit* in the "Spiritual Universe" (AN), which impinges its *Awareness* into the Physical Universe (KI), animating/controlling *Life* for its experience of *beta-existence* along an individual Alpha-Spirit's personal *Identity-continuum*, called a *ZU-line*.

81

Zu-Line : a theoretical construct in *Mardukite Zuism and Systemology* demonstrating *Spiritual Life Energy* (*ZU*) as a personal individual "continuum" of Awareness interacting with all Spheres of Existence on the Standard Model of Systemology; a spectrum of potential variations and interactions of a monistic continuum or singular *Spiritual Life Energy (ZU)* demonstrated on the Standard Model; an energetic channel of potential POV and "locations" of Beingness, demonstrated in early Systemology materials as an individual Alpha-Spirit's personal *Identity-continuum*, potentially connecting *Awareness (ZU)* of *Self* with "*Infinity*" simultaneous with all points considered in existence; a symbolic demonstration of the "*Life-line*" on which *Awareness (ZU)* extends from the direction of the "Spiritual Universe" (AN) in its true original *alpha state* through an entire possible range of activity resulting in its *beta state* and control of a *genetic-entity* occupying the *Physical Universe (KI)*.

Fundamentals of Systemology
in six
Basic Course Lesson Booklets

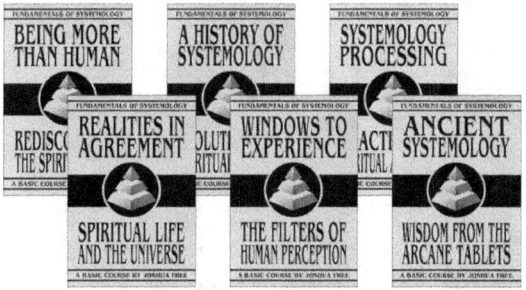

Also
available
as a
six-in-one
hardcover
edition!

THE SYSTEMOL

Seekers and students of the *Basic Course* and *Professional Course* will also be interested in the *Advanced Series* of the *Systemology Core.* These volumes are a complete chronological record of the Mardukite New Thought developments from the Systemology Society, published in 2019 through 2023.

The *Systemology Core* begins with the first professional publication released when the *Mardukite Systemology Society* emerged from the underground in 2019, with: *"The Tablets of Destiny Revelation."*

OGY PATHWAY

The Tablets of Destiny Revelation:
*How Long-Lost Anunnaki Wisdom
Can Change the Fate of Humanity*

Crystal Clear: *Handbook for Seekers*

Metahuman Destinations (*2 volumes*)

Imaginomicon:
Approaching Gateways to Higher Universes

Way of the Wizard: *Utilitarian Systemology*

Systemology-180: *Fast-Track to Ascension*

Systemology Backtrack:
Reclaiming Spiritual Power & Past-Life Memory

PUBLISHED BY THE **JOSHUA FREE** IMPRINT REPRESENTING

The Mardukite Academy of Systemology

THE JOSHUA FREE IMPRINT
JFI PUBLICATIONS

MARDUKITE
ZUISM

mardukite.com

www.ingramcontent.com/pod-product-compliance
Lightning Source LLC
Chambersburg PA
CBHW071214120626
46546CB00006B/2563